The Best
COOKIES

The Best
COOKIES

Snaps, Crescents, Bars, Drops,
and Other Crumbly Confections

By Gregg R. Gillespie

BLACK DOG
& LEVENTHAL
PUBLISHERS
NEW YORK

Published by
Black Dog & Leventhal Publishers, Inc.
151 West 19th Street
New York, NY 10011

Distributed by
Workman Publishing
708 Broadway
New York, NY 10003

Manufactured in Spain

ISBN 1-57912-293-0

Library of Congress Cataloging-in-Publication Data is on file and available
from Black Dog & Leventhal Publishers, Inc.

Cover and interior design by 27.12 Design, Ltd.
Interior layout by Sheila Hart Design, Inc.
Photography by Peter Barry

g f e d c b a

CONTENTS

ABERNATHY BISCUITS

Yield: 2 to 3 dozen

5½ cups all-purpose flour
1½ cups granulated sugar
1½ tsp. baking powder
1½ cups vegetable shortening

3 large eggs
3 tbsp. milk, or more if needed
3 tbsp. caraway seeds
1½ tsp. grated lemon zest

1. Preheat the oven to 375 degrees.
2. In a large bowl, combine the flour, sugar, and baking powder. Cut in the shortening until the mixture resembles coarse crumbs.
3. In another bowl, beat the eggs, milk, caraway seeds, and lemon zest until well blended. Blend into the dry ingredients until smooth. If the dough seems too stiff, add a little more milk 1 teaspoon at a time.
4. On a floured surface, roll out the dough ¼ inch thick. Using a 2-inch round cookie cutter, cut out cookies and place 1½ inches apart on ungreased baking sheets.
5. Bake for 7 to 10 minutes, until the edges are lightly browned. Transfer to wire racks to cool.

ALMOND CAKES

Yield: 5 to 6 dozen

2 large eggs
1 cup granulated sugar
½ tsp. vanilla extract

1 cup almonds, ground
1 cup all-purpose flour

1. Preheat the oven to 400 degrees. Lightly grease 2 baking sheets.
2. In a large bowl, beat the eggs until thick and light-colored. Beat in the sugar and vanilla extract. Beat in the almonds. Gradually blend in the flour.
3. Break off 1-inch pieces of dough and roll into balls. Place 2 inches apart on the prepared baking sheets.
4. Bake for 8 to 10 minutes, or until light golden color. Transfer to wire racks to cool.

Baking note: The balls of dough can be flattened and a half a glacé cherry or a nut pressed into each one before baking.

ALMOND CRESCENTS

Yield: 2 to 4 dozen

1 cup vegetable shortening
1 cup granulated sugar
1 large egg, separated
1 large egg yolk
4 hard-boiled large egg
   yolks, crumbled

1 tbsp. grated lemon zest
3 cups all-purpose flour
¼ cup almonds, ground
Granulated sugar for sprinkling

1. Preheat the oven to 350 degrees.
2. In a large bowl, cream the vegetable shortening and sugar until
   smooth. Beat in the egg yolks. Beat in the hard-boiled egg yolks one
   at a time, beating well after each addition. Beat in the lemon zest.
   Gradually blend in the flour.
3. In a medium bowl, beat the egg white until stiff but not dry.
4. Break off small pieces of dough and form into crescent shapes. Dip in the
   beaten egg white and place 1 inch apart on ungreased baking sheets.
5. Sprinkle the cookies with the almonds and sugar. Bake for 10 to 12
   minutes, until lightly colored. Transfer to wire racks and cool.

ALMOND TULIP
PASTRY CUPS

Yield: 2 to 3 dozen

¼ cup vegetable shortening
½ cup powdered sugar
2 large egg whites

¾ tsp. Amaretto liqueur
¼ cup all-purpose flour
⅓ cup almonds, ground fine

1. Preheat the oven to 425 degrees.
2. In a large bowl, cream the vegetable shortening and powdered sugar. Add the egg whites and Amaretto, beating until very smooth. Gradually blend in the flour. Fold in the almonds.
3. Drop 1 1/2 teaspoons of the batter 5 inches apart onto ungreased baking sheets. With the back of a spoon, spread into 4- to 5-inch rounds.
4. Bake for 5 to 6 minutes or until the edges are lightly browned. Using a spatula, remove the cookies from the sheets and place each cookie over an upside-down cup or glass. (If they have become too firm to shape, return briefly to the oven.) Let cool completely before removing.

Baking note: These are very easy to overbake; watch them closely. The cups can be used to hold fresh fruit, custards, or mousses. Or make smaller cups and fill them with whipped cream and sprinkle with shaved chocolate. (Do not fill the cookies until just before serving.) In an airtight container, the cups will keep well in the freezer for up to 6 months.

AMERICAN
OATMEAL CRISPS

Yield: 2 to 3 dozen

1¼ cups all-purpose flour
½ tsp. baking powder
½ tsp. baking soda
½ tsp. salt
1 cup vegetable shortening
¼ cup granulated sugar
1 cup packed light
  brown sugar

2 large eggs
¼ cup milk
1 tsp. almond extract
3 cups rolled oats
1 cup (6 oz.) semi-sweet, white
  chocolate, peanut butter, or
  butterscotch chips

1. Preheat the oven to 350 degrees
2. Combine the flour, baking powder, baking soda, and salt.
3. In a large bowl. Cream the vegetable shortening and both sugars.
   Beat in the eggs. Beat in the milk and almond extract. Gradually
   blend in the dry ingredients. Fold in the oats and chips.
4. Drop the dough by teaspoonfuls about 1½ inches apart onto
   ungreased baking sheets.
5. Bake for 10 to 12 minutes, until golden brown. Transfer to wire racks
   to cool.

AMERICAN SHORTBREAD

Yield: 8 dozen

2 cups (1 pound) butter, at
room temperature
1¾ cups granulated sugar

6 large eggs
1 tbsp. anise or caraway seeds
8 cups all-purpose flour

1. Preheat the oven to 400 degrees.
2. In a large bowl, cream the butter and sugar until light and fluffy.
3. In another bowl, beat the eggs until thick and light-colored. Beat the eggs into the butter mixture. Stir in the caraway seeds. Gradually blend in the flour.
4. On a floured surface, roll out the dough ¼ inch thick. Cut into 1-inch squares and place 1 inch apart on ungreased baking sheets.
5. Bake for 12 to 15 minutes, until lightly colored. Transfer to wire racks to cool.

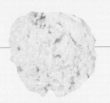

ANISE
COOKIES

Yield: 2 to 3 dozen

2¼ cups all-purpose flour
½ tsp. baking powder
¼ tsp. salt

2 large eggs
1½ cups granulated sugar
2 tsp. anise extract

1. Combine the flour, baking powder, and salt.
2. In a large bowl, beat the eggs until foamy. Beat in the sugar and the anise extract. Gradually blend in the dry ingredients. Cover and chill for at least 8 hours, or overnight.
3. Preheat the oven to 325 degrees. Grease 2 baking sheets.
4. Drop the dough by spoonfuls 1½ inches apart onto prepared baking sheets.
5. Bake for 10 to 12 minutes, until lightly colored. Transfer to wire racks to cool.

APPLE
COOKIES

Yield: 3 to 4 dozen

2 cups all-purpose flour
1 tsp. baking powder
½ tsp. ground nutmeg
1 tsp. ground cinnamon
½ tsp. ground cloves
½ tsp. salt
½ cup butter, at room temperature
1½ cups packed light brown sugar
1 large egg
¼ cup fresh lemon juice
1 tsp. vanilla extract

1 cup diced, peeled apples
1 cup walnuts, chopped
1 cup raisins
glaze
1½ cups powdered sugar
1 tbsp. butter at room temperature
2½ tbsp. evaporated milk
¼ tsp. vanilla extract
Pinch of salt

1. Preheat the oven to 400 degrees. Grease 2 baking sheets.
2. Combine the flour, baking powder, spices, and salt.
3. In a large bowl, cream the butter and brown sugar. Beat in the egg, lemon juice, and vanilla extract. Gradually blend in the dry ingredients. Fold in the apples, walnuts, and raisins.
4. Drop the dough by teaspoonfuls 1½ inches apart onto the prepared baking sheets. Bake for 12 to 15 minutes, or until golden brown.
5. Meanwhile, make the glaze: Combine all the ingredients in a small bowl and beat until smooth.
6. Transfer the cookies to wire racks. Spread the glaze over the tops of the warm cookies and let cool.

APPLE DROPS

Yield: 4 dozen

2 cups all-purpose flour
½ tsp. baking powder
½ tsp. baking soda
½ tsp. ground cinnamon
½ tsp. ground cloves

¼ tsp. ground nutmeg
½ cup vegetable shortening
4 large eggs
¾ cup frozen apple juice concentrate, thawed

1. Preheat the oven to 375 degrees. Grease 2 baking sheets.
2. In a large bowl, combine the flour, baking powder, baking soda, and spices. Cut in the vegetable shortening until mixture resembles fine crumbs.
3. In a medium bowl, beat the eggs until thick and light-colored. Beat in the apple juice concentrate. Add the dry mixture and blend to make a smooth dough.
4. Drop the dough by spoonfuls 1½ inches apart onto the prepared baking sheets.
5. Bake for 6 to 8 minutes, or until golden brown. Transfer to wire racks to cool.

APRICOT BARS

Yield: 2 to 4 dozen

2 cups all-purpose flour
2 tsp. baking powder
½ tsp. ground nutmeg
½ tsp. salt
2 tsp. grated orange zest

4 large eggs
2 cups granulated sugar
1½ cups dried apricots, diced
1 cup walnuts, chopped
Powdered sugar for sprinkling

1. Preheat the oven to 350 degrees. Grease a 13 by 9-inch baking pan.
2. Sift the flour, baking powder, nutmeg, and salt into a bowl. Stir in the orange zest.
3. In a large bowl, beat the eggs and sugar until thick and light-colored. Gradually blend in the dry ingredients. Fold in the apricots and walnuts.
4. Spread the batter evenly in the prepared pan. Bake for 15 to 20 minutes, until the top is golden, and a toothpick inserted into the center comes out clean.
5. Cool in the pan on a rack before cutting into large or small bars. Sprinkle with powdered sugar.

APRICOT CRESCENTS

Yield: 3 dozen

2 cups all-purpose flour
1 tsp. granulated sugar
Pinch of salt
1 cup vegetable shortening
1 cup sour cream

1 large egg
½ cup apricot preserves
½ cup walnuts, chopped
Powdered sugar for dusting

1. Combine the flour, sugar, and salt in a bowl. Cut in the vegetable shortening until the mixture resembles coarse crumbs. With a fork, stir in the sour cream and egg until a stiff dough forms. Cover and chill for at least 4 hours, or overnight.
2. Preheat the oven to 350 degrees. Grease 2 baking sheets.
3. Divide the dough into 3 pieces. On a floured surface, roll out each piece to an 11-inch round. Spread one-third of the apricot preserves evenly over each round, and sprinkle each round with one-third of the walnuts.
4. Cut each round into 12 wedges. Starting at the wide end, roll up each wedge. Place seam side down on the prepared baking sheets, placing the cookies about 1 inch apart and curving the ends to form crescent shapes.
5. Bake for 25 to 30 minutes, until lightly colored. Dust the warm cookies with powdered sugar and transfer to wire racks to cool.

APRICOT-SPICE COOKIES

Yield: 2 to 3 dozen

1 cup dried apricots
2 cups all-purpose flour
1 tsp. baking powder
1 tsp. ground allspice
½ tsp. ground cinnamon
½ tsp. salt
½ cup vegetable shortening

½ cup granulated sugar
1 tsp. baking soda
1 tbsp. warm water
1 large egg
1 cup golden raisins
1 cup pecans, chopped

1. Put the apricots through a food grinder, or grind them in a food processor or blender.
2. Combine the flour, baking powder, spices, and salt.
3. In a large bowl, cream the vegetable shortening and sugar.
4. Dissolve the baking soda in the warm water and add to the creamed mixture, beating until smooth. Beat in the egg. Gradually blend in the dry ingredients. Fold in the apricots, raisins, and pecans. Cover and chill for at least 1 hour.
5. Preheat the oven to 375 degrees. Grease 2 baking sheets.
6. Drop the dough by spoonfuls 1½ inches apart onto the prepared baking sheets.
7. Bake for 18 to 20 minutes, until browned on top. Transfer to wire racks to cool.

AUNT LIZZIE'S COOKIES

Yield: 5 to 6 dozen

3 cups all-purpose flour
1 tsp. baking powder
1 cup vegetable shortening
1½ cups granulated sugar
3 large eggs

1 tsp. vanilla extract
1 tsp. baking soda
2 tbsp. hot water
1 cup walnuts, chopped
1 cup raisins

1. Preheat the oven to 325 degrees. Grease 2 baking sheets.
2. Combine the flour and baking powder.
3. In a large bowl, cream the vegetable shortening and sugar until light and fluffy.
4. In another bowl, beat the eggs until thick and light-colored. Beat the eggs into the shortening mixture. Beat in the vanilla extract.
5. Dissolve the baking soda in the hot water and add to the egg mixture, beating until smooth. Gradually blend in the dry ingredients. Fold in the walnuts and raisins.
6. Drop the dough by the spoonfuls 1½ inches apart onto prepared baking sheets.
7. Bake for 10 to 12 minutes, until lightly colored. Transfer to wire racks to cool.

AUSTRIAN
WALNUT CRESCENTS
Yield: 4 to 6 dozen

1 cup vegetable shortening	2½ cups all-purpose flour
⅔ cup granulated sugar	¼ cup walnuts, chopped
2 tsp. vanilla extract	Powdered sugar for rolling

1. In a large bowl, cream the vegetable shortening and sugar. Beat in the vanilla extract. Gradually blend in the flour and nuts. Cover and chill for at least 4 hours.
2. Preheat the oven to 325 degrees.
3. Break off small pieces of the dough and form into crescent shapes, curving the ends. Place 1 inch apart on ungreased baking sheets.
4. Bake for 15 to 20 minutes, until the edges are a light brown. Transfer to wire racks to cool slightly.
5. Roll the warm cookies in powdered sugar to coat. Let cool on the racks.

Baking note: To make hazelnut crescents, an elegant variation, substitute hazelnut extract for the vanilla extract and chopped hazelnuts for the walnuts.

BACK BAY COOKIES

Yield: 2 to 3 dozen

2 cups all-purpose flour
¾ tsp. baking soda
1 tsp. ground cinnamon
¼ tsp. salt
⅔ cup butter, at room temperature

1 cup granulated sugar
2 large eggs
⅔ cup golden raisins
½ cup chestnuts, chopped

1. Preheat the oven to 350 degrees. Grease 2 baking sheets.
2. Combine the flour, baking soda, cinnamon, and salt.
3. In a large bowl, cream the butter and sugar. Beat in the eggs. Gradually blend in the dry ingredients. Fold in the raisins and chestnuts.
4. Drop the dough by spoonfuls 1 1/2 inches apart onto the prepared baking sheets.
5. Bake for 10 to 12 minutes, until lightly colored. Transfer to wire racks to cool.

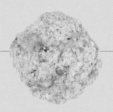

BANANA DROPS

1½ cups all-purpose flour
1 cup granulated sugar
½ tsp. baking soda
¾ tsp. ground cinnamon
¼ tsp. ground nutmeg
1 tsp. salt

¾ cup vegetable shortening
1 large egg
2 to 3 large bananas, mashed
1¾ cup rolled oats
2 cups (12 oz.) semi-sweet
    chocolate chips

1. Preheat the oven to 400 degrees.
2. Sift the flour, sugar, baking soda, cinnamon, nutmeg, and salt into a large bowl. Cut in the vegetable shortening. Stir in the egg and bananas until smooth. Fold in the oats and chocolate chips.
3. Drop the dough by spoonfuls 1½ inches apart onto ungreased baking sheets.
4. Bake for 12 to 15 minutes, until lightly colored. Transfer to wire racks to cool.

Baking notes: Raisins may be added to the dough. The chips can be of any type: semi-sweet or milk chocolate, butterscotch, or peanut butter.

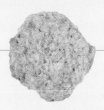

BANANA OATMEAL COOKIES

Yield: 3 to 5 dozen

1½ cups all purpose flour
½ tsp. baking soda
¾ tsp. ground cinnamon
¾ tsp. ground nutmeg
¼ tsp. salt
¾ cup vegetable shortening

1 cup granulated sugar
1 large egg
2 to 3 large bananas, mashed
1¾ cups rolled oats
½ cup almonds, chopped fine

1. Preheat the oven to 400 degrees.
2. Combine the flour, baking soda, cinnamon, nutmeg, and salt.
3. In a large bowl, cream the vegetable shortening and sugar. Beat in the egg and bananas. Gradually blend in the dry ingredients. Fold in the oats and almonds.
4. Drop the dough by spoonfuls 1½ inches apart onto ungreased baking sheets.
5. Bake for 12 to 15 minutes, until lightly colored. Transfer to wire racks and cool.

BANNOCKS
Yield: 4 to 6 dozen

1¼ cup rolled oats
¾ cup all-purpose flour
1 tbsp. granulated sugar
1 tbsp. baking powder

½ tsp. salt
5 tbsp. vegetable shortening
2 to 3 tbsp. water, or more as
  needed

1. Preheat the oven to 350 degrees.
2. Combine the rolled oats, flour, sugar, baking powder, and salt in a
   bowl. Using your fingertips, work in the vegetable shortening until the
   mixture resembles coarse crumbs. Add just enough water to turn the
   mixture into a smooth dough.
3. On a floured surface, roll out the dough ½ inch thick. Using a butter
   plate as a guide, cut out 6-inch circles and place 1 inch apart on
   ungreased baking sheets.
4. Bake for 18 to 20 minutes, until the Bannocks are slightly colored and
   firm to the touch. Transfer to wire racks to cool.

Baking note: Bannocks are usually served with jam or jelly.

BENNE
(SESAME SEED) COOKIES

Yield: 3 to 4 dozen

1 ¼ cups all-purpose flour
¼ tsp. baking powder
¼ tsp. salt
¾ cup butter, at room
   temperature

1 ½ cups packed light brown
   sugar
2 large eggs
1 tsp. vanilla extract
½ cup sesame seeds, toasted

1. Preheat the oven to 350 degrees. Grease 2 baking sheets.
2. Combine the flour, baking powder, and salt.
3. In a large bowl, cream the butter and sugar. Beat in the eggs and vanilla extract. Gradually blend in the dry ingredients. Fold in the sesame seeds.
4. Drop the dough by the spoonfuls 1 ½ inches apart onto the prepared baking sheets.
5. Bake for 10 to 12 minutes, until lightly colored. Transfer to wire racks to cool.

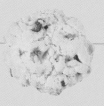

BILLY
GOATS

Yield: 5 to 6 dozen

4 cups all-purpose flour
1 tbsp. plus 1 tsp. baking
  powder
1 tsp. ground allspice
1 cup walnuts, chopped
½ tsp. salt
1 cup vegetable shortening
2 cups granulated sugar

4 large eggs
1 tsp. vanilla extract
1 tsp. baking soda
1 tbsp. warm water
1 cup sour cream
1½ cups dates, pitted and
  chopped

1. Preheat the oven to 350 degrees. Grease 2 baking sheets.
2. Combine the flour, baking powder, allspice, and salt.
3. In a large bowl, cream the vegetable shortening and sugar. Beat in the vanilla extract.
4. Dissolve the baking soda in the warm water and add to the egg mixture, beating until smooth.
5. Drop the dough by spoonfuls 1½ inches apart onto prepared baking sheets.
6. Bake for 12 to 15 minutes, until golden. Transfer to wire racks to cool.

BIRD'S NEST
COOKIES

Yield: 3 to 4 dozen

2 cups all-purpose flour
¼ tsp. salt
1 cup vegetable shortening
½ cup granulated sugar
1 large egg, separated

1 large egg yolk
1½ tsp. vanilla extract
1 cup walnuts, chopped
Chocolate kisses for garnish

1. Preheat the oven to 375 degrees.
2. Combine the flour and salt.
3. In a large bowl, cream the vegetable shortening and sugar. Beat in the egg yolks and vanilla extract. Gradually blend in the dry ingredients.
4. In a shallow bowl, beat the egg white until frothy. Spread the walnuts on waxed paper.
5. Break off 1-inch pieces of dough and roll into balls. Dip the balls in the egg white to coat, then roll in the walnuts and place 1 inch apart on ungreased baking sheets.
6. With your finger, make a small depression in the center of each cookie. Bake for 12 to 15 minutes, until lightly colored.
7. Press an upside-down chocolate kiss into the center of each hot cookie, and transfer to wire racks to cool.

BISCOTTI

Yield: 3 to 4 dozen

2 cups all-purpose flour	6 tbsp. vegetable shortening
½ cup granulated sugar	4 large eggs
½ tsp. baking powder	½ cup walnuts, chopped

1. Preheat the oven to 350 degrees. Grease 2 baking sheets.
2. In a medium bowl, combine the flour, sugar, and baking powder. Cut in the vegetable shortening until the mixture resembles coarse crumbs.
3. In a large bowl, beat the eggs until thick and light-colored. Gradually beat the eggs into the flour mixture. Fold in the walnuts.
4. On a floured surface, roll out the dough ¼ inch thick. Using a cookie cutter, cut into shapes and place 1½ inches apart on the prepared baking sheets.
5. Bake for 12 to 14 minutes, until lightly colored. Transfer to wire racks to cool.

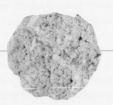

BLACKBERRY
COOKIES

Yield: 4 to 5 dozen

2 cups all-purpose flour	1 large egg
2 tsp. baking powder	¼ cup milk
½ tsp. salt	1½ tsp. grated lemon zest
½ cup vegetable shortening	1 cup blackberry purée,
1 cup granulated sugar	unstrained

1. Combine the flour, baking powder, and salt.
2. In a large bowl, cream the vegetable shortening and sugar. Beat in the egg and milk. Beat in the lemon zest. Gradually blend in the dry ingredients. Fold in the blackberry purée. Cover and chill for at least 4 hours.
3. Preheat the oven to 375 degrees.
4. Drop the dough by spoonfuls 1½ inches apart onto ungreased baking sheets.
5. Bake for 12 to 15 minutes, until lightly colored. Transfer to wire racks to cool.

Baking note: You can make these with fresh blackberries instead of the purée. Rinse and thoroughly dry fresh berries. Add the berries to the flour mixture, tossing them gently to coat thoroughly.

BLACK WALNUT
REFRIGERATOR COOKIES

Yield: 8 to 9 dozen

2⅔ cups all-purpose flour
2 tsp. baking powder
¼ tsp. salt
¾ cup butter, at room
temperature

1½ cups packed light brown
sugar
2 large eggs
1 tsp. vanilla extract
1½ cups black walnuts,
chopped

1. Combine the flour, baking powder, and salt.
2. In a large bowl, cream the butter and brown sugar. Beat in the eggs
and vanilla extract. Gradually blend in the dry ingredients. Fold in the
walnuts. Cover and refrigerate just until firm enough to shape, about
30 minutes.
3. Divide the dough into 3 pieces. Form each piece into a log about 8
inches long. Wrap in waxed paper and chill for at least 24 hours.
4. Preheat the oven to 375 degrees. Grease 2 baking sheets.
5. Slice the logs into ¼ inch thick slices and place 1 inch apart on the
prepared baking sheets.
6. Bake for 8 to 10 minutes, until lightly colored. Transfer to wire racks
to cool.

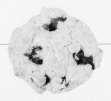

BLUEBERRY
COOKIES

Yield: 4 to 5 dozen

2 cups all-purpose flour	1 large egg
2 tsp. baking powder	¼ cup milk
½ tsp. salt	1 tsp. almond extract
½ cup vegetable shortening	1½ tsp. grated lemon zest
1 cup granulated sugar	1 cup blueberries

1. Combine the flour, baking powder, and salt.
2. In a large bowl, cream the vegetable shortening and sugar. Beat in the egg. Beat in the milk, almond extract, and lemon zest. Gradually blend in the dry ingredients. Fold in the blueberries.
3. Cover and chill for at least 4 hours.
4. Preheat the oven to 375 degrees.
5. Drop the dough by spoonfuls about 1 inch apart onto ungreased baking sheets. Bake for 12 to 15 minutes, until lightly colored. Transfer to wire racks to cool.

BLUSHING COOKIES

Yield: 2 to 3 dozen

2 cups all-purpose flour
1 cup walnuts, chopped fine
½ tsp. ground cinnamon

½ cup vegetable shortening
¾ cup powdered sugar
Red jimmies for sprinkling

1. Preheat the oven to 400 degrees.
2. Combine the flour, walnuts, and cinnamon.
3. In a large bowl, cream the vegetable shortening and powdered sugar until light and fluffy. Gradually blend in the dry ingredients.
4. On a floured surface, roll out the dough ¼ inch thick. Using cookie cutter, cut into shapes and place on ungreased baking sheets. Sprinkle the jimmies over the tops of the cookies.
5. Bake for 8 to 10 minutes, until lightly colored. Transfer to wire racks to cool.

BONBONS

Yield: 3 dozen

1½ cups all-purpose flour
½ tsp. salt
½ cup vegetable shortening
½ cup powdered sugar

2 tbsp. heavy cream
2 tsp. vanilla extract
36 candied glacé cherries

1. Preheat the oven to 350 degrees.
2. Combine the flour and salt.
3. In a large bowl, cream the vegetable shortening and powdered sugar. Beat in the cream and vanilla extract. Gradually blend in the dry ingredients.
4. Break off pieces of dough and flatten each one on a floured surface into a round about 3 to 4 inches in diameter. Place a candied cherry in the center of each round and wrap the dough up around the cherry. Pinch to seal. Place 1 inch apart on ungreased baking sheets.
5. Bake for 8 to 10 minutes, until the dough is set (see Baking note). Transfer to wire racks to cool.

Baking note: To decorate, dip the top of each ball into sugar icing or melted chocolate.

BOURBON
CHEWS

Yield: 3 to 4 dozen

1 cup all-purpose flour
1 tsp. ground ginger
½ tsp. salt
½ cup molasses

¼ cup vegetable shortening
2 tbsp. bourbon
½ cup packed light brown sugar
¼ cup walnuts, chopped

1. Preheat the oven to 325 degrees. Lightly grease 2 baking sheets.
2. Combine the flour, ginger, and salt together.
3. In a small saucepan combine the molasses and vegetable shortening and heat over low heat, stirring until smooth. Remove from the heat and add the bourbon. Beat in the brown sugar. Gradually blend in the dry ingredients. Fold in the walnuts.
4. Drop the dough by spoonfuls onto the prepared baking sheets.
5. Bake for 10 to 12 minutes, until lightly colored. Transfer to wire racks to cool.

BOW
COOKIES

Yield: 4 to 5 dozen

3 large eggs
3 tbsp. granulated sugar
¼ tsp. salt
1 tbsp. vanilla extract

3 cups all-purpose flour
Vegetable oil for deep-frying
Powdered sugar for sprinkling

1. In a large bowl, beat the eggs until thick and light-colored. Beat in the sugar and salt. Beat in the vanilla extract. Gradually blend in the flour.
2. On a floured surface, roll out the dough 1/8-inch thick. Cut into strip 6 inches by 1 1/2 inches. Make a 3/4-inch-long slit down the center of each strip and pull one end of the strip through the slit to form a bow tie.
3. In a deep-fryer or deep, heavy pot, heat the oil to 375 degrees. Fry the cookies, in batches, until golden brown. Drain on a wire rack lined with paper towels, then sprinkle with powdered sugar.

Baking notes: Colored sugar crystals can be used to create colored bows for the holidays. For a distinctive look, use a pastry wheel to cut the strips.

BRANDY COOKIES

Yield: 1 to 3 dozen

1 cup vegetable shortening
½ cup granulated sugar
1 tbsp. brandy

¼ cup unsweetened cocoa powder
3 cups all-purpose flour

1. Preheat the oven to 350 degrees.
2. In a large bowl, cream the vegetable shortening and sugar. Beat in the brandy. Blend in the cocoa powder. Gradually blend in the flour.
3. Place the dough in a cookie press or a pastry bag fitted with a plain round tip. Press or pipe the dough onto ungreased baking sheets, spacing the cookies 1 1/2 inches apart.
4. Bake for 8 to 10 minutes, until light golden. Transfer to wire racks to cool.

Baking notes: These cookies are usually formed using a plain round tip, but you can experiment with other shapes. This dough keeps well in the refrigerator; it also freezes well. It can also be rolled out 1/4-inch thick and cut into shapes with cookie cutters. For variation, use candied fruit to decorate the cookies.

BROWN SUGAR
SAND TARTS

Yield: 3 to 5 dozen

¾ cup all-purpose flour
¼ tsp. baking powder
¼ tsp. salt
¼ cup butter, at room
temperature

⅓ cup packed light brown sugar
1 large egg
½ tsp. vanilla extract
Light brown sugar for sprinkling

1. Combine the flour, baking powder, and salt.
2. In a large bowl, cream the butter and brown sugar. Beat in the egg.
   Beat in the vanilla extract. Gradually blend in the dry ingredients.
   Cover and chill for 2 hours.
3. Preheat the oven to 375 degrees. Lightly grease 2 baking sheets.
4. On a floured surface, roll out the dough to a thickness of ⅛ inch.
   With cookie cutters, cut into shapes and place 1 inch apart on prepared baking sheets. Sprinkle with brown sugar and lightly press the
   sugar into the cookie.
5. Bake for 8 to 10 minutes, until firm to the touch. Transfer to wire
   racks to cool.

BROWN-EYED
SUSANS

Yield: 4 to 5 dozen

1¾ cups all-purpose flour
¼ tsp. salt
¾ cup vegetable shortening
½ cup granulated sugar

1 large egg
1 tsp. vanilla extract
7 oz. milk chocolate, chopped

1. Combine the flour and salt.
2. In a large bowl, cream the vegetable shortening and sugar. Beat in the egg. Beat in the vanilla extract. Gradually blend in the dry ingredients. Cover and chill for 1 hour.
3. Preheat the oven to 400 degrees.
4. Melt the milk chocolate in the top half of a double boiler over low heat, stirring until smooth. Remove from the heat; keep warm over hot water.
5. Break off small pieces of the dough and roll into balls. Place 1½ inches apart on ungreased baking sheets. Press your finger into the center of each ball to make a slight indentation.
6. Bake for 8 to 10 minutes, until lightly colored. Spoon a little of the melted milk chocolate into the center of each hot cookie and transfer to wire racks to cool.

BUTTER
COOKIES I

Yield: 2 to 3 dozen

1 cup butter, at room
  temperature
½ cup granulated sugar
1 large egg yolk
½ tsp. almond extract

2⅓ cups all-purpose flour
½ cup almonds, ground fine
1 large egg white, lightly beaten
Jam or preserves for filling

1. In a large bowl, cream the butter and sugar. Beat in the egg yolk.
   Beat in the almond extract. Gradually blend in the flour. Cover and
   chill for 12 hours.
2. Preheat the oven to 350 degrees.
3. On a floured surface, roll out the dough to a thickness of 1¼ inch.
   Using a 2-inch round cookie cutter, cut into circles. Using a ½ inch
   round cookie cutter, cut out the centers of one half of the cookies.
   Place the cookies 1½ inches apart on ungreased baking sheets. Brush
   the cut-out cookies with beaten egg white and sprinkle the ground
   almonds over the top.
4. Bake for 8 to 10 minutes until lightly colored. Transfer to wire racks
   to cool.
5. Spread a layer of jam or preserves over the plain cookies and top with
   the cut-out cookies.

BUTTER
COOKIES II

Yield: 6 to 8 dozen

1 cup butter
4 cups all-purpose flour

3 large eggs
2 cups granulated sugar

1. Preheat the oven to 350 degrees.
2. Melt the butter in a large saucepan. Remove from heat and add 2 cups of the flour all at once. Beat in the eggs one at a time. Beat in the sugar. Gradually blend in the remaining flour.
3. On a floured surface, roll out the dough to a thickness of ¼ inch. Using cookie cutters, cut into shapes and place the cookies 1½ inches apart on ungreased baking sheets.
4. Bake for 12 to 15 minutes, until lightly colored. Transfer to wire racks to cool.

BUTTERSCOTCH
COOKIES

Yield: 3 to 5 dozen

2 cups all-purpose flour
½ tsp. baking soda
½ tsp. salt
¾ cup vegetable shortening
1 cup packed light brown sugar

2 large eggs
1 cup (6 oz.) rolled oats
½ cup almonds, chopped
1 cup butterscotch chips

1. Preheat the oven to 350 degrees. Lightly grease 2 baking sheets.
2. Combine the flour, baking soda, and salt.
3. In a large bowl, cream the vegetable shortening and brown sugar.
   Beat in the eggs. Gradually blend in the dry ingredients. Fold in the
   oats and almonds. Fold in the butterscotch chips.
4. Drop the dough by spoonfuls 2 inches apart onto the prepared
   baking sheets.
5. Bake for 10 to 12 minutes, until lightly browned. Transfer to wire
   racks to cool.

CAROB CHIP
OATMEAL COOKIES

Yield: 2 to 3 dozen

2½ cups all-purpose flour
1 tbsp. baking soda
¼ tsp. salt
1 cup vegetable shortening
¼ cup honey

2 large eggs
2 cups rolled oats
¾ cup carob chips
1 cup golden raisins
1 cup walnuts, chopped

1. Preheat the oven to 350 degrees. Lightly grease 2 baking sheets.
2. Combine the flour, baking soda, and salt.
3. In a large saucepan, melt the vegetable shortening with the honey, stirring until smooth. Remove from the heat and beat in the eggs one at a time. Gradually blend in the dry ingredients. Fold in the oats, carob chips, raisins, and walnuts.
4. Drop the dough by spoonfuls 1½ inches apart onto the prepared baking sheets.
5. Bake for 12 to 15 minutes, until golden brown. Transfer to wire racks to cool.

CASHEW
SHORTBREAD

Yield: 4 to 5 dozen

4½ cups all-purpose flour
1 cup cashews, ground fine

2 cups vegetable shortening
2½ cups packed light
brown sugar

1. Preheat the oven to 350 degrees.
2. Combine the flour and cashews.
3. In a large bowl, cream the vegetable shortening and brown sugar.
   Gradually blend in the dry ingredients.
4. Pinch off small pieces of dough and roll into balls. Place 1 inch apart
   on ungreased baking sheets. Flatten the balls with the bottom of a
   glass dipped in flour.
5. Bake for 10 to 15 minutes, until lightly colored. Transfer to wire racks
   to cool.

CHOCOLATE CHIP
COOKIES I

Yield: 6 to 7 dozen

2¼ cups all-purpose flour
1 tsp. baking soda
1 package vanilla-flavored
   instant pudding
1 cup vegetable shortening
¼ cup granulated sugar

¾ cup packed light brown sugar
2 large eggs
1 tsp. vanilla extract
1½ cups (9 oz.) semi-sweet
   chocolate chips
1 cup walnuts, chopped fine

1. Preheat the oven to 375 degrees.
2. Combine the flour, baking soda, and vanilla pudding.
3. In a large bowl, cream the vegetable shortening and the two sugars.
   Beat in the vanilla extract. Gradually blend in the dry ingredients. Fold
   in the chocolate chips and walnuts.
4. Drop the dough by spoonfuls 1½ inches apart onto ungreased
   baking sheets.
5. Bake for 8 to 10 minutes, until lightly colored. Transfer to wire racks
   to cool.

Baking note: For chocolate chocolate chip cookies, use a chocolate
instant pudding in place of the vanilla pudding.

CHOCOLATE CHIP
COOKIES II

Yield: 3 to 5 dozen

2 cups all-purpose flour
1 tsp. baking soda
½ tsp. salt
1 cup vegetable shortening
½ cup granulated sugar

¾ packed light brown sugar
1 large egg
2½ tsp. white crème de menthe
1⅓ cups (8 oz.) semi-sweet
    chocolate chips

1. Combine the flour, baking soda, and salt.
2. In a large bowl, cream the vegetable shortening and the two sugars. Beat in the egg and crème de menth. Gradually blend in the dry ingredients. Fold in the chocolate chips. Cover and refrigerate for 1 hour.
3. Preheat the oven to 350 degrees. Lightly grease 2 baking sheets.
4. Drop the dough by spoonfuls 1½ inches apart onto the prepared baking sheets.
5. Bake for 10 to 12 minutes, until lightly colored. Transfer to wire racks to cool.

CHOCOLATE CRINKLES

Yield: 3 to 4 dozen

2 cups all purpose flour	1½ cups granulated sugar
2 tsp. baking powder	2 large eggs
3 oz. semi-sweet chocolate, chopped	¼ cup milk
	1 tsp. vanilla extract
½ cup canola oil	Powdered sugar for rolling

1. Preheat the oven to 350 degrees. Lightly grease 2 baking sheets.
2. Combine the flour and baking powder.
3. Melt the chocolate in a double boiler over low heat, stirring until smooth. Remove from the heat.
4. In a large bowl, beat the canola oil and sugar until well blended. Beat in the eggs one at a time, beating well after each addition. Beat in the chocolate. Beat in the milk and vanilla extract. Gradually blend in the dry ingredients.
5. Pinch off walnut-sized pieces of dough and roll into balls. Roll in powdered sugar and place 1½ inches apart on prepared baking sheets.
6. Bake for 12 to 15 minutes, or until firm to the touch. Roll in powdered sugar while still warm and transfer to wire racks to cool.

CHOCOLATE-FILLED PINWHEELS

Yield: 4 to 5 dozen

2 cups all-purpose flour
1 tsp. baking powder
½ tsp. salt
¾ cup vegetable shortening
1 cup granulated sugar
1 large egg
1 tbsp. vanilla extract

filling
1 cup (6 oz.) semi-sweet
    chocolate chips
2 tbsp. butter
1 cup walnuts, ground fine
½ tbsp. vanilla extract

1. Combine the flour, baking powder, and salt.
2. Cream the vegetable shortening and sugar in a large bowl. Beat in the egg. Beat in the vanilla extract. Gradually blend in the dry ingredients. Measure out ⅔ cup of the dough and set aside. Cover the remaining dough and chill for 2 hours.
3. To make the filling, melt the chocolate and butter in the top of a double boiler over low heat, stirring until smooth. Remove from the heat and stir in the walnuts and vanilla extract. Blend in the reserved dough.
4. On a floured surface, roll out the chilled dough to a 16- by 12-inch rectangle. Spread the chocolate mixture over the dough to within ¼ inch of the edges. Starting on a long side, roll the dough up jelly-roll fashion. Pinch the seam to seal. Cut in half to make two 8-inch logs. Wrap in waxed paper and chill overnight.
5. Preheat the oven to 350 degrees.
6. Slice the logs into ¼-inch-thick slices and place 1½ inches apart on ungreased baking sheets.
7. Bake for 10 to 12 minutes, until lightly colored. Transfer to wire racks to cool.

CHOCOLATE
SANDWICHES

Yield: 3 to 4 dozen

1¼ cups all-purpose flour	1 cup granulated sugar
1 cup walnuts, ground fine	1 tsp. vanilla extract
½ tsp. salt	¾ cup semi-sweet chocolate
⅔ cup vegetable shortening	chips

1. Preheat the oven to 400 degrees. Lightly grease 2 baking sheets.
2. Combine the flour, walnuts, and salt.
3. In a large bowl, cream the vegetable shortening and sugar. Beat in the vanilla. Gradually blend in the dry ingredients.
4. On a floured surface, roll out the dough to a thickness of ⅛ inch. Using a 2-inch fluted round cookie cutter, cut the dough into rounds and place 1 inch apart on the prepared baking sheets.
5. Bake for 8 to 10 minutes, until firm to the touch. Transfer to wire racks to cool.
6. Melt the chocolate in a double boiler over low heat, stirring until smooth. Spread a thin layer of chocolate on the bottom half of the cookies and top with the remaining cookies to form sandwich cookies.

CHRISTMAS COOKIES

Yield: 5 to 6 dozen

2 cups all-purpose flour
1 tsp. baking soda
¼ tsp. salt
½ cup vegetable shortening
⅔ cup packed light
   brown sugar
1 large egg
¼ cup cider vinegar

1½ tsp. rum
½ cup candied citrus peel,
   chopped fine
½ cup red and green
   glacé cherries
1 large egg white, beaten
¼ cup slivered almonds for
   the topping

1. Combine the flour, baking soda, and salt.
2. In a large bowl, cream the vegetable shortening and brown sugar.
   Beat in the egg. Beat in the vinegar. Beat in the rum. Gradually blend
   in the dry ingredients. Fold in the coconut, candied citrus peel, and
   glacé cherries. Cover and chill for 8 hours or overnight.
3. Preheat the oven to 350 degrees. Lightly grease 2 baking sheets.
4. Working with one quarter of the dough at a time, pinch off walnut-
   sized pieces of dough and roll into balls. Place 2 inches apart on the
   prepared baking sheets. Flatten each ball with the bottom of a glass
   dipped in flour, then brush the cookies with the beaten egg white
   and sprinkle with the slivered almonds.
5. Bake for 8 to 10 minutes, until lightly colored. Transfer to wire racks
   to cool.

CHRISTMAS
WREATHS

Yield: 3 to 4 dozen

1 cup vegetable shortening
½ cup granulated sugar
1 large egg
1 tsp. vanilla extract
2½ tbsp. all-purpose flour

1⅓ cups almonds, ground fine
¼ cup maple syrup
Red and green glacé cherries,
   halved

1. Preheat the oven to 350 degrees. Lightly grease 2 baking sheets.
2. In a large bowl, cream the vegetable shortening and sugar. Beat in the egg and vanilla extract. Gradually blend in the flour. Transfer one-third of the dough to a medium bowl.
3. Fill a cookie press or a pastry bag fitted with a small star tip with the remaining dough and press or pipe out small rings onto the prepared baking sheets, spacing them 1 inch apart.
4. Add the almonds and maple syrup to the reserved cookie dough and blend well. Place ¼ to ½ teaspoon of this filling in the center of each ring, and place a half cherry at the point where the ends of each ring join.
5. Bake for 10 to 12 minutes, until lightly colored. Transfer to wire racks to cool.

CINNAMON
CRISPS

Yield: 3 to 4 dozen

1¼ cups all-purpose flour	1 large egg
1 tsp. baking soda	1 tsp. almond extract
¼ tsp. salt	½ cup almonds, chopped fine
½ cup vegetable shortening	2 tsp. ground cinnamon
1 cup granulated sugar	

1. Preheat the oven to 375 degrees. Lightly grease 2 baking sheets.
2. Combine the flour, baking soda, and salt.
3. In a large bowl, cream the vegetable shortening and sugar. Beat in the egg. Beat in the almond extract. Gradually blend in the dry ingredients.
4. Combine the almonds and cinnamon in a shallow dish.
5. Pinch off walnut-sized pieces of dough and roll into balls. Roll in the almond mixture and place 1½ inches apart on the prepared baking sheets.
6. Bake for 10 to 12 minutes, until lightly colored. Transfer to wire racks to cool.

COCONUT
KISSES
Yield: 2 to 3 dozen

4 large egg whites	1 cup granulated sugar
¼ tsp. cream of tartar	¼ tsp. almond extract
¼ tsp. salt	1½ cups flaked coconut

1. Preheat the oven to 250 degrees. Line 2 baking sheets with parchment paper.
2. In a large bowl, beat the egg whites until foamy. Beat in the cream of tartar and salt. Beat in the sugar a tablespoon at a time. Beat in the almond extract until the whites hold stiff peaks. Gently fold in the coconut.
3. Drop the mixture by spoonfuls 1½ inches apart onto the prepared baking sheets.
4. Bake for 35 to 45 minutes, until firm to the touch. Transfer to wire racks to cool.

Baking note: For crisper kisses, when the cookies are done, turn the oven off and let them cool completely in the oven.

COFFEE-FLAVORED
MOLASSES COOKIES

Yield: 3 to 5 dozen

4½ cups all-purpose flour
2 tsp. ground ginger
2 tsp. ground cinnamon
1 cup vegetable shortening
1 cup granulated sugar
1 large egg

1 tbsp. plus 1 tsp. baking soda
¼ cup hot water
1 cup molasses, warmed
¾ cup strong brewed coffee

1. Preheat the oven to 375 degrees. Lightly grease 2 baking sheets.
2. Combine the flour, ginger, and cinnamon.
3. In a large bowl, cream the vegetable shortening and sugar. Beat in the egg.
4. Dissolve the baking soda in the hot water and add to the egg mixture, beating until smooth. Beat in the molasses and coffee. Gradualy blend in the dry ingredients.
5. Drop the dough by spoonfuls 1½ inches apart onto the prepared baking sheets.
6. Bake for 8 to 10 minutes, until just starting to color. Transfer to a wire rack to cool.

COFFEE KISSES

Yield: 2 to 3 dozen

1 tbsp. plus 1 tsp. instant
  coffee powder
1 tbsp. boiling water
4 large egg whites

¼ tsp. cream of tartar
¼ tsp. salt
1 cup granulated sugar
1 tsp. crème de cacao

1. Preheat the oven to 250 degrees. Line 2 baking sheets with parchment paper.
2. In a cup, dissolve the coffee powder in the boiling water. Let cool.
3. In a large bowl, beat the egg whites until foamy. Beat in the cream of tartar and salt. Beat in the sugar 1 tablespoon at a time. Beat in the crème de cacao and beat until the whites form stiff peaks. Fold in the coffee.
4. Drop the dough by spoonfuls 1 inch apart onto the prepared baking sheets.
5. Bake for 35 to 45 minutes, until firm to the touch. Cool completely on the baking sheets on wire racks.

COOKIE
PIZZA

Yield: 4 dozen

crust
¾ cup all-purpose flour
½ tsp. baking powder
½ tsp. baking soda
Pinch of salt
½ cup vegetable shortening
¾ cup packed light brown sugar
1 large egg

1 tsp. vanilla extract
1 cup rolled oats
½ cup flaked coconut
topping
1 cup (6 oz.) semi-sweet
  chocolate chips
1 cup walnuts, chopped
½ cup M&Ms®

1. Preheat the oven to 350 degrees. Lightly grease a 14- to 15-inch pizza pan.
2. Combine the flour, baking powder, baking soda, and salt.
3. In a large bowl, cream the vegetable shortening and brown sugar. Beat in the egg and vanilla. Gradually blend in the dry ingredients. Fold in the oats and coconut.
4. Press the dough evenly into the prepared pan. Sprinkle the chocolate chips and walnuts evenly over the top.
5. Bake for 12 to 15 minutes, until lightly colored. Sprinkle the M&Ms over the hot cookies. Cool in the pan on a wire rack for a few minutes before cutting into wedges.

CRANBERRY COOKIES

Yield: 3 to 4 dozen

1½ cups all-purpose flour
½ tsp. baking powder
¼ tsp. salt
½ cup vegetable shortening
¾ cup powdered sugar
3 tbsp. milk

1 tsp. Amaretto liqueur
¾ cup cranberries, fresh or
   dried, chopped fine (see
   Baking note)
½ cup flaked coconut

1. Combine the flour, baking powder, and salt.
2. In a large bowl, cream the vegetable shortening and powdered sugar. Beat in the milk and Amaretto. Gradually blend in the dry ingredients. Fold in the cranberries.
3. Divide the dough in half. Form each half into a log 1½ inches in diameter. Roll in coconut. Wrap in waxed paper and chill for 8 hours.
4. Preheat the oven to 375 degrees.
5. Cut the logs into ¼ -inch-thick slices and place each slice 1 inch apart on ungreased baking sheets.
6. Bake for 12 to 15 minutes, until lightly colored. Transfer to wire racks to cool.

Baking note: If using dried cranberries, cover cranberries with boiling water and plump for 10 minutes before chopping.

CREAM CHEESE
REFRIGERATOR COOKIES

Yield: 2 to 3 dozen

1 cup all-purpose flour
3 tbsp. poppy seeds
¼ tsp. salt

4 oz. cream cheese, at room
   temperature
⅓ cup canola oil
¼ cup honey, warmed

1. Combine the flour, poppy seeds, and salt.
2. In a large bowl, beat the cream cheese, oil, and honey until well
   blended and smooth. Gradually blend in the dry ingredients. Shape
   the dough into a log 2½ inches in diameter. Wrap in waxed paper
   and chill for 4 hours.
3. Preheat the oven to 400 degrees. Lightly grease 2 baking sheets.
4. Cut the log into ¼-inch-thick slices and place 1 inch apart on prepared baking sheets.
5. Bake for 6 to 8 minutes, or until lightly browned. Transfer to wire
   racks to cool.

CREAM CHEESE TASTIES

Yield: 3½ dozen

2 cups all-purpose flour
¼ tsp. salt
1 cup vegetable shortening
8 oz. cream cheese, at room
temperature

½ cup powdered sugar
About ¼ cup raspberry
preserves
Powdered sugar for sprinkling

1. Combine the flour and salt.
2. In a large bowl, beat the vegetable shortening, cream cheese, and powdered sugar until smooth. Gradually blend in the dry ingredients. Divide the dough in half. Wrap each half in waxed paper and chill for 8 hours.
3. Preheat the oven to 375 degrees.
4. On a floured surface, roll out one-half of the dough to a rectangle approximately 10 inches by 11½ inches. Trim the edges of the dough and cut lengthwise into 4 strips. Cut each strip into 5 squares. Place 1/4 teaspoon raspberry preserves in the center of each square and fold the dough over to form a triangle. Press the edges together to seal and place 1 inch apart on ungreased baking sheets. Repeat with the other half of the dough.
5. Bake for 10 to 12 minutes, until lightly colored. Sprinkle with powdered sugar and transfer to wire racks to cool.

CUT-OUT
HANUKKAH COOKIES
Yield: 3 to 4 dozen

2½ cups all-purpose flour
1¼ tsp. baking powder
⅛ tsp. salt
¼ cup canola oil
¾ cup powdered sugar

1 large egg
¼ cup milk
1 tsp. vanilla extract
1 tsp. grated lemon zest
Vanilla icing

1. Combine the flour, baking powder, and salt.
2. In a large bowl, beat the oil and sugar. Beat in the egg. Beat in the milk and vanilla extract. Beat in the lemon zest. Gradually blend in the dry ingredients. Cover and chill for 6 hours.
3. Preheat the oven to 350 degrees.
4. On a floured surface, roll out the dough to a thickness of ⅛ inch. Using cookie cutters, cut into shapes and place 1½ inches apart on ungreased baking sheets.
5. Bake for 6 to 8 minutes, until lightly colored. Transfer to wire racks to cool before decorating with the icing.

DATE
DROPS

Yield: 1 to 2 dozen

1¼ cups all-purpose flour
½ tsp. baking powder
½ tsp. baking soda
¼ cup vegetable shortening
¾ cup packed light brown sugar
1 large egg

½ cup sour cream
1 pound dates, pitted and
  chopped
About ½ cup walnuts
Vanilla icing

1. Preheat the oven to 400 degrees. Lightly grease 2 baking sheets.
2. Combine the flour, baking powder, baking soda, and salt.
3. In a large bowl, cream the vegetable shortening and brown sugar.
   Beat in the egg and sour cream. Gradually blend in the dry ingredients.
   Fold in the dates.
4. Drop the dough by spoonfuls 1½ inches apart onto the prepared
   baking sheets. Press a walnut into the center of each of cookie.
5. Bake for 8 to 10 minutes, until lightly colored. Transfer to wire racks
   to cool.
6. Fill a pastry bag fitted with a small plain tip with the icing and pipe a
   ring of icing around each walnut.

EASY FUDGE
COOKIES

Yield: 6 to 7 dozen

2 oz. semi-sweet chocolate, chopped
4⅓ cups all-purpose flour
1 tsp. baking powder
½ tsp. baking soda
¼ tsp. salt
1 cup vegetable shortening

1 cup packed light brown sugar
1 cup granulated sugar
2 large eggs
⅓ cup milk
1 tsp. vanilla extract
½ cup walnuts, chopped (optional)

1. Melt the chocolate in a double boiler over low heat, stirring until smooth. Remove from the heat.
2. Combine the flour, baking powder, baking soda, and salt.
3. In a large bowl, cream the vegetable shortening and two sugars. Beat in the eggs one at a time. Beat in the milk and vanilla extract. Beat in the melted chocolate. Gradually blend in the dry ingredients. Fold in the walnuts.
4. Divide the dough in half. Form each half into 2-inch-thick logs. Wrap in waxed paper and chill for 8 hours or overnight.
5. Preheat the oven to 375 degrees.
6. Cut the logs into ⅛-inch-thick slices and place 1 inch apart on ungreased baking sheets.
7. Bake for 12 to 15 minutes, until lightly colored. Transfer to wire racks to cool.

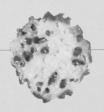

FLORENTINES

Yield: 2 to 4 dozen

¾ cup almonds, ground fine
¼ cup all-purpose flour
¼ cup butter
⅓ cup granulated sugar
5 tbsp. heavy cream

½ cup grated orange zest
topping
4 oz. semi-sweet chocolate,
  chopped
3 tbsp. butter

1. Preheat the oven to 375 degrees. Lightly grease and flour 2 baking sheets.
2. Combine the almonds and flour.
3. Combine the butter, sugar, and cream in a saucepan and bring to a
   boil. Remove from the heat and gradually blend in the dry ingredients.
   Stir in the orange zest. The mixture will be very thin.
4. Drop the batter by tablespoonfuls 3 inches apart onto the prepared
   baking sheets. With the back of a spoon dipped in flour, spread the
   batter into 2-inch rounds.
5. Bake for 12 to 15 minutes, until the edges start to brown (the centers
   may still look bubbly). Cool on the baking sheet on wire racks.
6. For the topping, melt the chocolate and butter in the top of a double
   boiler, stirring until smooth. Remove from the heat.
7. Place the cooled cookies upside down on the wire racks. Using a
   pastry brush, paint a thin layer of the melted chocolate over the
   bottom of each one. Let cool until the chocolate sets.

FRUIT
DROPS

1 cup cornflakes, crushed
2 cups shredded coconut
½ tsp. salt
1 cup sweetened
   condensed milk
1 cup dates, pitted and
   chopped fine

1 cup pitted prunes,
   chopped fine
1 cup figs, chopped fine
1 cup golden raisins,
   chopped fine
1 cup currants

1. Preheat the oven to 350 degrees. Lightly grease 2 baking sheets.
2. In a large bowl, combine the cornflakes, coconut, and salt. Stir in the
   condensed milk. Stir in all the fruit and blend thoroughly.
3. Drop the mixture by spoonfuls 1 inch apart onto the prepared
   baking sheets.
4. Bake for 12 to 15 minutes, until golden colored. Transfer to wire racks
   to cool.

GINGER
COOKIES
Yield: 8 to 10 dozen

6½ cups all-purpose flour
1 tsp. ground ginger
1 tsp. ground cinnamon
¼ tsp. ground cloves
2 tsp. salt

1 cup vegetable shortening
1 cup packed light brown sugar
2 tsp. baking soda
½ tsp. warm water
1½ cups molasses

1. Combine the flour, spices, and salt.
2. In a large bowl, cream the vegetable shortening and brown sugar.
3. Dissolve the baking soda in the warm water and add to the creamed
   mixture, beating until smooth. Beat in the molasses. Gradually blend
   in the dry ingredients. Cover and chill for 24 hours.
4. Preheat the oven to 350 degrees. Lightly grease 2 baking sheets.
5. On a floured surface, roll out the dough to a thickness of ¼ inch.
   Using a 1¾ -inch round cookie cutter, cut out cookies and place 1½
   inches apart on the prepared baking sheets.
6. Bake for 10 to 12 minutes, until dry-looking and firm to the touch.
   Transfer to wire racks to cool.

GINGERBREAD CRINKLES

Yield: 4 to 5 dozen

2 cups all-purpose flour
2 tsp. baking soda
1 tsp. ground cinnamon
1 tsp. ground ginger
¼ tsp. salt

1 cup granulated sugar
⅔ cup canola oil
1 large egg
¼ cup molasses, warmed
Granulated sugar for rolling

1. Preheat the oven to 350 degrees.
2. Combine the flour, baking soda, spices, and salt.
3. In a large bowl, beat the sugar and the oil together. Beat in the egg.
   Beat in the molasses. Gradually blend in the dry ingredients.
4. Pinch off walnut-sized pieces of dough and roll into balls. Roll in granulated sugar until well coated and place the balls 3 inches apart on
   ungreased baking sheets.
5. Bake for 12 to 15 minutes, until lightly colored. Transfer to wire racks
   to cool.

GREEN WREATHS

Yield: 2 to 3 dozen

6 tbsp. vegetable
  shortening
32 marshmallows
½ tsp. vanilla extract

½ tsp. almond extract
½ tsp. green food coloring
4 cups cornflakes, crushed
Red cinnamon candy

1. Line 2 baking sheets with waxed paper.
2. In the top of a double boiler, melt the vegetable shortening with the
   marshmallows. Add the vanilla and almond extracts. Stir in the food
   coloring. Remove from the heat and stir in the cornflakes. Replace
   over bottom half of double boiler to keep warm.
3. Drop the mix by tablespoonful 2 inches apart onto the prepared baking sheets. With well-oiled hands, form the batter into wreath shapes.
   Decorate with cinnamon candy and chill until set.

HAZELNUT CRESCENTS

Yield: 2 to 3 dozen

¾ cup butter, at room temperature
½ cup granulated sugar
½ tsp. almond extract

½ tsp. vanilla extract
2 cups all-purpose flour
½ cup hazelnuts, chopped fine
Powdered sugar for rolling

1. Preheat the oven to 300 degrees.
2. In a large bowl, cream the butter and sugar. Beat in the almond and vanilla extracts. Gradually blend in the flour. Fold in the hazelnuts. The dough will be stiff.
3. Pinch off walnut-sized pieces of dough and form each one into a crescent shape. Place 1½ inches apart on ungreased baking sheets.
4. Bake for 15 minutes, until lightly colored. Roll in powdered sugar and transfer to wire racks to cool.

HONEY CHEWS
Yield: 3 to 5 dozen

2 cups whole wheat flour	1 cup canola oil
1 cup soy flour	½ cup molasses
1 cup rolled oats	1 tbsp. fresh orange juice
¼ tsp. salt	½ tsp. coffee liqueur
1 cup honey	1 cup flaked coconut

1. Preheat the oven to 350 degrees. Lightly grease 2 baking sheets.
2. Combine the two flours, the oats, and salt.
3. In a large saucepan, combine the honey, oil, molasses, and orange juice and heat gently, stirring until well blended. Remove from the heat and stir in the coffee liqueur. Transfer to a large bowl, and gradually blend in the dry ingredients. Stir in the coconut.
4. Drop the dough by spoonfuls 1½ inches apart onto the prepared baking sheets.
5. Bake for 10 to 12 minutes, until lightly colored. Transfer to wire racks to cool.

LEMON WAFERS

Yield: 4 to 5 dozen

1 cup vegetable shortening
1 cup granulated sugar
4 large egg yolks
2 tbsp. fresh lemon juice

1 tbsp. lemon extract
3 cups all-purpose flour
Orange- or yellow-colored
    sugar crystals for sprinkling

1. In a large bowl, cream the vegetable shortening and sugar. Beat in the egg yolks. Beat in the lemon juice and lemon extract. Gradually blend in the flour. Cover and chill for 4 hours.
2. Preheat the oven to 350 degrees. Lightly grease 2 baking sheets.
3. On a floured surface, roll out the dough to a thickness of ⅛ inch. Using a 1½-inch round cookie cutter, cut into rounds and place 1 inch apart on the prepared baking sheets. Sprinkle with colored sugar crystals.
4. Bake for 10 to 12 minutes, until lightly colored. Transfer to wire racks to cool.

LOVE
LETTERS
Yield: 4 to 5 dozen

filling
2 large egg whites
¼ cup granulated sugar
½ tsp. ground cinnamon
1 cup almonds, ground fine
1 tsp. grated lemon zest

2 cups all-purpose flour
¼ tsp. salt
¾ cup vegetable shortening
2 tbsp. granulated sugar
4 large egg yolks

1. Preheat the oven to 350 degrees.
2. To make the filling, in a medium bowl, beat the egg whites until stiff but not dry. Beat in the sugar and cinnamon. Fold in the almonds and the lemon zest. Set aside.
3. Combine the flour and salt.
4. In a large bowl, cream the vegetable shortening and sugar. Beat in the egg yolks. Gradually blend in the dry ingredients.
5. On a floured surface, roll out the dough to a thickness of ¼ inch. Using a sharp knife, cut into 3-inch squares. Place 1 inch apart on ungreased baking sheets. Drop a teaspoonful of the filling into the center of each square and fold the corners into the center like an envelope. Lightly seal the seams.
6. Bake for 18 to 20 minutes, until lightly colored. Transfer to wire racks to cool.

MACADAMIA NUT COOKIES

Yield: 2 to 3 dozen

3 cups all-purpose flour
2 tsp. baking soda
1 tsp. salt
1½ cups vegetable shortening
1½ cups packed light
  brown sugar
⅔ cup granulated sugar

4 large eggs
1 tsp. vanilla extract
1 tsp. fresh lemon juice
2 cups macadamia nuts,
  chopped
½ cup rolled oats

1. Combine the flour, baking soda, and salt.
2. In a large bowl, cream the vegetable shortening and two sugars. Beat in the eggs one at a time, beating well after each addition. Beat in the vanilla extract and lemon juice. Gradually blend in the dry ingredients. Fold in the macadamia nuts and oats. Cover and chill for 4 hours.
3. Preheat the oven to 325 degrees. Lightly grease 2 baking sheets.
4. Drop the dough by spoonfuls 1½ inches apart onto the prepared baking sheets.
5. Bake for 15 to 18 minutes, until lightly colored. Transfer to wire racks to cool.

MACAROON NUT
WAFERS

Yield: 1 to 2 dozen

2 large egg whites
¼ tsp. salt
½ cup powdered sugar

1 tsp. Amaretto liqueur
1 cup almonds, ground fine

1. Preheat the oven to 350 degrees. Line 2 baking sheets with parchment paper.
2. In a medium bowl, beat the egg whites with the salt until they form stiff peaks. Fold in the powdered sugar. Fold in the Amaretto. Fold in the almonds.
3. Drop the dough by spoonfuls 1½ inches apart onto the prepared baking sheets.
4. Bake for 15 to 20 minutes, until lightly colored. Cool slightly on the pans, then transfer to wire racks to cool completely.

MANDELBROT

Yield: 3 to 4 dozen

3 cups all-purpose flour
1 tsp. baking powder
¼ tsp. salt
½ cup honey, warmed
6 tbsp. butter, at room
    temperature

3 large eggs
½ tsp. grated lemon zest
½ cup pistachio nuts, chopped
1 tsp. anise seeds, crushed

1. Preheat the oven to 350 degrees.
2. Combine the flour, baking powder, and salt.
3. In a large bowl, beat the honey and butter together. Beat in the eggs one at a time, beating well after each addition. Beat in the lemon zest. Gradually blend in the dry ingredients. Stir in the pistachio nuts and anise seeds.
4. Divide the dough in half. Shape each half into a loaf 12 inches long, 3 inches wide, and 1½–2 inches high. Place the logs on an ungreased baking sheet, leaving 1½ inches between them.
5. Bake for 25 to 30 minutes, until lightly colored and firm to the touch.
6. Transfer the loaves to a cutting board and cut into ½-inch-thick slices. Place 1 inch apart on the baking sheets and bake for 5 to 7 minutes longer, or until the slices are lightly toasted. Transfer to wire racks to cool.

MEXICAN
WEDDING CAKES
Yield: 3 dozen

¾ cup vegetable shortening
¼ cup granulated sugar
1 tsp. vanilla extract

2 cups all-purpose flour
½ cup walnuts, chopped
Powdered sugar for rolling

1. Preheat the oven to 200 degrees. Lightly grease 2 baking sheets.
2. In a large bowl, cream the shortening and sugar together. Beat in the vanilla extract. Gradually blend in the flour. Fold in the walnuts.
3. Pinch off walnut-sized pieces of dough and roll into balls. Place 1 inch apart on the prepared baking sheets.
4. Bake for 25 to 35 minutes, or until golden. Roll in powdered sugar and transfer to wire racks to cool.

MINT
CHOCOLATE COOKIES

Yield: 3 to 4 dozen

3 cups all-purpose flour
1½ cups walnuts, ground
½ tsp. baking soda
½ tsp. salt
1 cup vegetable shortening
1 cup granulated sugar

½ cup packed light brown sugar
2 large eggs
1 tsp. vanilla extract
14 oz. mint-chocolate wafer
    candies, chopped

1. Combine the flour, walnuts, baking soda, and salt.
2. In a large bowl, cream the vegetable shortening and two sugars. Beat in the eggs. Beat in the vanilla extract. Gradually blend in the dry ingredients. Fold in the mint wafers. Cover and chill for 4 hours.
3. Preheat the oven to 350 degrees.
4. Drop the dough by spoonfuls 1½ inches apart onto ungreased baking sheets.
5. Bake for 10 to 12 minutes, until lightly colored. Transfer to wire racks to cool.

OATMEAL
COCONUT CRISPS

Yield: 4 to 5 dozen

1 cup all-purpose flour
1 tsp. baking powder
½ tsp. baking soda
¼ tsp. salt
¾ cup vegetable shortening

1⅔ cups granulated sugar
2 large eggs
1½ tsp. vanilla extract
2½ cups rolled oats
1 cup flaked coconut

1. Preheat the oven to 375 degrees. Lightly grease 2 baking sheets.
2. Combine the flour, baking powder, baking soda, and salt.
3. In a large bowl, cream the vegetable shortening and sugar. Beat in the eggs. Beat in the vanilla. Gradually blend in the dry ingredients. Fold in the oats and coconut.
4. Drop the dough by spoonfuls 3 inches apart onto the prepared baking sheets.
5. Bake for 12 to 14 minutes, until golden brown. Transfer to wire racks to cool.

OATMEAL CRISPS

Yield: 2 to 3 dozen

1¼ cups all-purpose flour
½ tsp. baking powder
½ tsp. baking soda
½ tsp. salt
1 cup vegetable shortening
¼ cup granulated sugar

1 cup packed light brown sugar
2 large eggs
¼ tsp. milk
1 tsp. vanilla extract
3 cups rolled oats
1 cup (6 oz.) chocolate chips

1. Preheat the oven to 350 degrees.
2. Combine the flour, baking powder, baking soda, and salt.
3. In a large bowl, cream the vegetable shortening and two sugars. Beat
   in the eggs. Beat in the milk and vanilla extract. Gradually blend in
   the dry ingredients. Fold in the oats and chocolate chips.
4. Drop the dough by spoonfuls 1½ inches apart onto ungreased
   baking sheets.
5. Bake for 10 to 12 minutes, until lightly colored. Transfer to wire racks
   to cool.

OATMEAL
THINS

Yield: 2 to 3 dozen

1 cup rolled oats	1 cup granulated sugar
2 tsp. baking powder	2 large eggs
½ tsp. salt	1 tsp. vanilla extract
1 tbsp. vegetable shortening	

1. Preheat the oven to 350 degrees. Lightly grease 2 baking sheets.
2. Combine the oats, baking powder, and salt.
3. In a large bowl, cream the shortening and sugar. Beat in the eggs. Beat in the vanilla extract. Gradually blend in the dry ingredients.
4. Drop the dough by spoonfuls 2 inches apart onto the prepared baking sheets.
5. Bake for 12 to 15 minutes, until lightly colored. Transfer to wire racks to cool.

OLD-FASHIONED
SOFT GINGER COOKIES

Yield: 4 to 5 dozen

4 cups all-purpose flour
2 tsp. baking soda
1 tbsp. ground ginger
1 tsp. salt

¾ cup vegetable shortening
2 cups packed light brown sugar
⅔ cup molasses
⅔ cup boiling water

1. Combine the flour, baking soda, ginger, and salt.
2. In a large bowl, cream the vegetable shortening and brown sugar. Add in the molasses and boiling water, beating until smooth. Gradually blend in the dry ingredients. Cover and chill for at least 6 hours.
3. Preheat the oven to 350 degrees. Lightly grease 2 baking sheets.
4. On a floured surface, roll out the dough to a thickness of ¼ inch. Using a 2-inch round cookie cutter, cut the cookies and place 1 inch apart on the prepared baking sheets.
5. Bake for 18 to 20 minutes, until lightly colored. Transfer to wire racks to cool.

PEANUT BUTTER
JUMBO COOKIES

Yield: 2 to 3 dozen

2½ cups all-purpose flour
1 tsp. baking powder
1½ tsp. baking soda
2 cups packed light brown sugar

1 cup vegetable shortening
1 cup peanut butter
2 large eggs

1. Preheat the oven to 350 degrees. Lightly grease 2 baking sheets.
2. Combine the flour, baking powder, and baking soda.
3. In a large bowl, beat together the brown sugar, vegetable shortening, peanut butter, and eggs. Gradually blend in the dry ingredients. The dough will be very soft.
4. Using a serving spoon, drop the dough by spoonfuls 3 inches apart onto the prepared baking sheets. Using the back of a spoon dipped in flour, spread the cookies into large rounds.
5. Bake for 10 to 12 minutes, until golden brown. Cool on the baking sheets on wire racks.

PECAN CRISPIES

Yield: 2 to 3 dozen

2 cups all-purpose flour
2 tsp. baking powder
½ tsp. salt
1½ cups vegetable shortening
1 cup granulated sugar

2 large eggs
1 tsp. vanilla extract
¾ cup pecans, chopped
Powdered sugar

1. Combine the flour, baking powder, and salt.
2. In a large bowl, cream the vegetable shortening and sugar. Beat in the eggs. Beat in the vanilla extract. Gradually blend in the dry ingredients. If the dough seems too dry, add a little water ½ teaspoonful at a time. Cover and chill for 4 hours.
3. Preheat the oven to 350 degrees.
4. Pinch off walnut-sized pieces of the dough and roll into balls. Roll in the chopped pecans and place 1½ inches apart on ungreased baking sheets. Flatten each ball with the bottom of a glass dipped in powdered sugar.
5. Bake for 6 to 8 minutes, until lightly colored. Cool slightly on the baking sheets, then transfer to wire racks to cool completely.

PEPPERMINT DELIGHTS

Yield: 4 to 5 dozen

1½ cups all-purpose flour
½ tsp. salt
1 cup vegetable shortening
1 cup powdered sugar

2 tsp. vanilla extract
1 cup rolled oats
¼ cup peppermint candies,
   crushed fine

1. Preheat the oven to 325 degrees.
2. Combine the flour and salt.
3. In a large bowl, cream the vegetable shortening and powdered sugar.
   Beat in the vanilla extract. Gradually blend in the dry ingredients. Fold
   in the oats. Fold in the candies.
4. On a floured surface, roll out the dough to a thickness of ¼ inch.
   Using a 1½-inch round cookie cutter, cut out the cookies and place 1
   inch apart on ungreased baking sheets.
5. Bake for 10 to 12 minutes, until lightly colored. Transfer to wire racks
   to cool.

RUGELACH

Yield: 2 to 3 dozen

1 cup butter, at room
   temperature
8 oz. cream cheese, at room
   temperature
6 tbsp. powdered sugar
1 tbsp. raspberry-
   flavored brandy

2¾ cups all-purpose flour
filling
¾ cup packed light brown sugar
½ cup almonds, chopped
½ cup raisins, plumped in
   warm water and drained
1 tsp. ground cinnamon

1. Combine the butter, cream cheese, and powdered sugar in a large
   bowl and beat until smooth and creamy. Beat in the brandy. Gradually
   blend in the flour. Divide the dough into 4 pieces. Wrap the dough in
   waxed paper and chill for 4 hours.
2. Preheat the oven to 350 degrees. Lightly grease 2 baking sheets.
3. To make the filling, combine all the ingredients in a small bowl and
   toss to mix.
4. On a floured surface, roll out each piece of dough into a 9-inch circle.
   Spread one-quarter of the filling over each round. Cut each round into 8
   wedges. Starting at the wide end, roll up each wedge. Place 1 inch apart
   on the prepared baking sheets, curving the ends to form crescents.
5. Bake for 20 to 25 minutes, until lightly colored. Transfer to wire racks
   until cool.

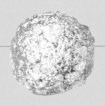

RUM
BALLS
Yield: 3 to 5 dozen

2½ cups crushed gingersnaps   1½ cups pecans, ground fine
½ cup honey   Powdered sugar for rolling
6 tbsp. rum

1. In a large bowl, combine all of the ingredients and stir to form a sticky dough. Pinch off small pieces of dough and roll into balls. Roll each ball in powdered sugar.
2. Store in an airtight container for at least 1 week before serving. Before serving, roll the balls a second time in powdered sugar.

RUM-TOPPED
GINGER COOKIES

Yield: 3 to 4 dozen

2 cups all-purpose flour
⅔ cup granulated sugar
2 tsp. ground ginger
Pinch of salt
½ cup butter, chilled and cut into small pieces
½ cup large-curd cottage cheese
1 large egg white, beaten with 2 tsp. water for egg glaze

Colored sugar crystals

topping
1½ cups butter, at room temperature
3 cups powdered sugar
1 tbsp. minced crystallized ginger
3 tbsp. rum

1. Preheat oven to 350 degrees. Lightly grease 2 baking sheets.
2. In a large bowl, combine the flour, sugar, ginger, and salt. Cut in the butter until the mixture resembles coarse bread crumbs. Blend in the cottage cheese. The dough will be stiff. If the dough is too dry, add a little water 1 teaspoonful at a time. Cover and chill for 30 minutes.
3. On a floured surface, roll out dough to a thickness of ⅛ inch. Using a 2-inch round or 2-inch scalloped cookie cutter, cut out cookies. Place 1 inch apart on the prepared baking sheets and brush with egg glaze. Sprinkle with the sugar crystals.
4. Bake for 10 to 12 minutes, or until browned around the edges. Transfer to wire racks to cool.
5. To make the topping, cream the butter and sugar in a small bowl. Beat in the ginger and rum. Spread over the top of the cooled cookies.

Baking note: The ginger flavor will be more intense if the cookies are stored in an airtight container.

SNICKER DOODLES

Yield: 3 to 4 dozen

3 cups all-purpose flour
2 tsp. baking powder
¼ tsp. salt
1 cup vegetable shortening
1⅓ cups granulated sugar

2 large eggs
1 tsp. vanilla extract
3 tbsp. granulated sugar
2 tbsp. ground cinnamon

1. Preheat the oven to 350 degrees. Lightly grease 2 baking sheets.
2. Combine the flour, baking powder, and salt.
3. In a large bowl, cream the vegetable shortening and sugar. Beat in the eggs. Beat in the vanilla extract. Gradually blend in the dry ingredients.
4. In a small bowl, combine the sugar and cinnamon.
5. Pinch off 1-inch pieces of dough and roll into balls. Roll each ball in the cinnamon sugar and place 1 inch apart on the prepared baking sheets.
6. Bake for 10 to 12 minutes, until lightly colored. Transfer to wire racks to cool.

SPICE
CONES

Yield: 5 to 6 dozen

¾ cup all-purpose flour
1½ tsp. ground ginger
1½ tsp. ground nutmeg
6 tbsp. vegetable shortening

½ cup packed light brown sugar
¼ cup molasses
1 tbsp. brandy

1. Preheat the oven to 350 degrees.
2. Combine the flour and spices.
3. In a large bowl, cream the vegetable shortening and sugar. Beat in the molasses and brandy. Gradually blend in the dry ingredients.
4. Drop the dough by spoonfuls 2½ inches apart onto ungreased baking sheets.
5. Bake for 5 to 6 minutes, until golden brown. As soon as the cookies are cool enough to handle, remove them from the baking sheet and roll up around metal cone shapes. Place seam side down on wire racks to cool.

Baking note: You will need metal cone forms for this recipe; they are available in specialty cookware shops. If the cookies harden before you are able to form them, reheat them for about 30 seconds in the oven. These cones can be filled with many types of dessert toppings or ice cream. If you are filling them with ice cream, chill the cones in the freezer for at least 30 minutes before filling them — if you fill the cookies too soon, they will soften before they are served.

TOSCA COOKIES

Yield: 3 to 4 dozen

1 cup all-purpose flour
⅓ cup almonds, ground
⅓ cup farina cereal
½ tsp. baking powder
1 cup vegetable shortening
⅔ cup granulated sugar

1 large egg
glaze
4 tbsp. butter, melted
6 tbsp. granulated sugar
1 tsp. corn syrup
⅓ cup slivered almonds

1. Combine the flour, almonds, farina, and baking powder.
2. In a large bowl, cream the vegetable shortening and sugar. Beat in the egg. Gradually blend in the dry ingredients. Cover and chill for 2 hours.
3. Preheat the oven to 350 degrees. Lightly grease baking sheets.
4. To make the glaze, combine the butter, sugar, and corn syrup in a small bowl and beat until smooth.
5. Drop the dough by spoonfuls 1½ inches apart onto the prepared baking sheets.
6. Bake for 10 to 12 minutes, just until lightly colored. Brush the cookies with the glaze, sprinke with the slivered almonds, and bake for 5 minutes longer. Transfer to wire racks to cool.

TRAIL MIX
COOKIES

Yield: 3 to 4 dozen

¾ cup all-purpose flour
½ tsp. baking soda
½ cup vegetable shortening
1 cup packed light brown sugar
½ cup peanut butter
1 large egg

1 tsp. vanilla extract
1 cup (6 oz.) semi-sweet
   chocolate chips
1 cup raisins
⅔ cup peanuts, chopped

1. Preheat the oven to 375 degrees. Lightly grease 2 baking sheets.
2. Combine the flour and baking soda.
3. In a large bowl, cream the vegetable shortening and brown sugar.
   Beat in the peanut butter. Beat in the egg and vanilla extract.
   Gradually blend in the dry ingredients. Fold in the chocolate chips,
   raisins, and peanuts.
4. Drop the dough by spoonfuls 1½ inches apart onto the prepared
   baking sheets.
5. Bake for 10 to 12 minutes, until lightly colored. Transfer to wire racks
   to cool.
6. When the cookies are cool, wrap individually and store in an
   airtight container.

VICEROYS
Yield: 4 to 6 dozen

3 cups all-purpose flour
1 cup pecans, ground fine
1½ tsp. baking powder
1½ cups vegetable shortening

1½ cups granulated sugar
2 large eggs
2 tsp. Tía Maria liqueur
⅓ cup warm water

1. Preheat the oven to 350 degrees. Lightly grease 2 baking sheets.
2. Combine the flour, pecans, and baking powder.
3. In a large bowl, cream the vegetable shortening and sugar. Beat in the eggs one at a time. Beat in the Tía Maria and water. Gradually blend in the dry ingredients.
4. Drop the dough by spoonfuls 1½ inches apart onto prepared baking sheets.
5. Bake for 12 to 15 minutes, until lightly colored. Transfer to wire racks to cool.

VIRGINIA REBELS

Yield: 3 to 4 dozen

1 cup all-purpose flour
6 tbsp. unsweetened
   cocoa powder
½ tsp. baking soda
½ tsp. salt
1¼ cups vegetable shortening

1½ cups granulated sugar
1 large egg
¼ cup water
½ tsp. whiskey
3 cups rolled oats

1. Preheat the oven to 350 degrees.
2. Combine the flour, cocoa powder, baking soda, and salt.
3. In a large bowl, cream the vegetable shortening and sugar. Beat in the egg. Beat in the water and the whiskey. Gradually blend in the dry ingredients. Stir in the oats.
4. Drop the dough by spoonfuls 1½ inches apart onto ungreased baking sheets.
5. Bake for 10 to 12 minutes, or until lightly colored. Transfer to wire racks to cool.

WHEAT FLAKE JUMBLES

Yield: 3 to 4 dozen

1 cup all-purpose flour
½ tsp. baking powder
¼ tsp. baking soda
¼ tsp. salt
⅓ cup vegetable shortening
½ cup packed light brown
   sugar

1 large egg
1½ tbsp. sour milk
1 tsp. vanilla extract
½ cup dates, pitted and
   chopped fine
½ cup walnuts, chopped
1½ cups wheat flakes

1. Preheat the oven to 375 degrees. Lightly grease 2 baking sheets.
2. Combine the flour, baking powder, baking soda, and salt.
3. In a large bowl, cream the vegetable shortening and brown sugar. Beat in the egg. Beat in the sour milk and vanilla extract. Gradually blend in the dry ingredients. Fold in the dates and walnuts.
4. Spread the cornflakes in a pie plate.
5. Drop the dough by spoonfuls onto the wheat flakes until completely coated. Place 3 inches apart on the prepared baking sheets.
6. Bake for 12 to 15 minutes, until golden brown. Transfer to wire racks to cool.

WHOOPIE
PIES

Yield: 3 to 4 dozen

2 cups all-purpose flour
6 tbsp. carob powder
2 tsp. baking powder
½ tsp. salt
⅓ cup vegetable shortening
1 cup powdered sugar
1 large egg
1 cup skim milk

1 tsp. crème de cacao
½ cup white chocolate chips
filling
¾ cup vegetable shortening
1 cup powdered sugar
1 tsp. coffee liqueur
½ cup store-bought
marshmallow topping

1. Preheat the oven to 375 degrees. Lightly grease 2 baking sheets.
2. Combine the flour, carob powder, baking powder, and salt.
3. In a large bowl, cream the vegetable shortening and powdered sugar.
   Beat in the egg. Beat in the milk and crème de cacao. Gradually blend
   in the dry ingredients. Fold in the chocolate chips.
4. Drop the dough by heaping tablespoonfuls 3 inches apart onto the
   prepared baking sheets.
5. Bake for 7 to 10 minutes, until a toothpick inserted in the center
   comes out clean. Transfer to wire racks to cool.
6. To make the filling, beat the vegetable shortening and powdered sugar in a
   medium bowl. Beat in the coffee liqueur. Beat in the marshmallow topping.
7. To assemble, cut the cookies horizontally in half. Spread the filling lib-
   erally over the bottoms and sandwich with the tops.

Baking note: To make more uniform cookies, you can use crumpet or
muffin rings to form the pies.

ZUCCHINI BARS

Yield: 2 to 3 dozen

2½ cups all-purpose flour
1 tsp. ground cinnamon
½ cup granulated sugar
½ cup vegetable oil
2 large eggs

¾ cup finely chopped zucchini
½ cup mashed, cooked carrots
1 cup pecans, chopped
⅓ cup raisins

1. Preheat the oven to 350 degrees. Lightly grease and flour a 13 by 9-inch baking pan.
2. Combine the flour and cinnamon.
3. In a large bowl, beat the sugar and vegetable oil together. Beat in the eggs one at a time. Beat in the zucchini and carrots. Gradually blend in the dry ingredients. Stir in the pecans and raisins. Spread the batter evenly in the prepared baking pan.
4. Bake for 20 to 25 minutes, until a toothpick inserted in the center comes out clean. Cool in the pan on a wire rack before cutting into large or small bars.

ZWIEBACK

Yield: 2 to 3 dozen

1½ cups all-purpose flour
½ cup almonds, ground
1½ tsp. baking powder
½ cup vegetable shortening

½ cup granulated sugar
2 large eggs
2 tsp. Amaretto liqueur

1. Preheat the oven to 325 degrees.
2. Combine the flour, almonds, and baking powder.
3. In a large bowl, cream the vegetable shortening and sugar. Beat in the eggs one at a time. Beat in the Amaretto. Gradually blend in the dry ingredients.
4. Shape the dough into a loaf 13 inches long and 2½ inches wide and place on an ungreased baking sheet.
5. Bake for 18 minutes, or until firm to the touch.
6. Transfer the loaf to a cutting board and cut into ½-inch-thick slices. Cut each slice in half diagonally. Place the slices on the baking sheets and bake for 20 minutes. Turn off the oven and leave the cookies in the oven 20 minutes longer; do not open the oven door. Transfer to wire racks to cool.